W9-DEZ-018

In The Wild

Chimpanzees

Claire Robinson

Produced by Times, Malaysia
Designed by Celia Floyd
Cover design by Lucy Smith

01 00 99 98 97
10 9 8 7 6 5 4 3 2 1

ISBN 1-57572-136-8

Library of Congress Cataloging-in-Publication Data

Robinson, Claire, 1955-
    Chimpanzees / Claire Robinson.
      p.   cm. -- (In the wild)
    Includes bibliographical references (p.   ) and index.
    Summary: Describes a family of chimpanzees living in Africa,
covering what they eat, how they care for their young, how they
comunicate, and more.
    ISBN 1-57572-136-8 (lib. bdg.)
    1. Chimpanzees--Juvenile literature.   [1. Chimpanzees.]
    I. Title. II. Series: Robinson, Claire, 1955-   In the wild.
    QL737.P96R6   1997
    599. 885--dc21   97-12313
                                      CIP
                                      AC

Acknowledgements

The author and publishers are grateful to the following for permission to reproduce copyright
photographs:
ARDEA London Ltd, p.5 left (Jean-Paul Ferrero), pp.11, 22 (Adrian Warren);
BBC Natural History Unit/Gerry Ellis, p.9;
Bruce Coleman Ltd, p.15 (Peter Davey), p.4 right (Jorg & Petra Wegner);
NHPA/Jeff Goodman, p.5 right;
Oxford Scientific Films, pp.4, 7, 10, 16 (Mike Birkhead), pp.13, 14, 17, 18, 19, 20, 21, 23 (Clive
Bromhall), p.12 (Jackie Le Févre/Survival), p.6 (Michael W. Richards), p.8 (Richard Smithers).

Cover photograph: Oxford Scientific Films

Special thanks to Oxford Scientific Films

Some words are shown in bold, **like this**. You can find out what they mean by looking in
the glossary.

Contents

Chimpanzee Relatives

Chimpanzees, or chimps, are a type of **ape**. The animals you see here are all apes.

chimpanzee

gibbon

gorilla

orangutan

Apes have long, strong arms. Unlike monkeys, they don't have a tail.

What's it like to live in a family of chimpanzees?

Where Chimps Live

Chimpanzees live in central and west Africa. They like hot **tropical** forests and grasslands.

Their hands and arms are strong for
climbing and swinging from tree to tree.
Their feet have thumbs, which help
them to grip branches.

The Family

Chimpanzees belong to very large families—between 10 and 80 animals in one family group. They enjoy doing things together.

These chimps are **grooming** each other gently with their fingers. Grooming helps the **apes** to make friends in the group. It is also restful.

Night and Day

During the day, most chimpanzees travel on the ground. Notice how they walk on their feet and their **knuckles**.

At night they climb up into the trees to
sleep. They bend branches and leaves
to make a comfortable nest.

Eating

This mother and her baby have gone off by themselves to look for food. Chimps like seeds, young leaves, and insects.

But most of all, they enjoy the taste of ripe fruit. They spend up to four hours a day searching for this delicious food.

Sticks and Stones

Sometimes nuts and fruit have a hard
shell. The clever apes use stones
to break them open.

Ants and **termites** are a treat too! This female carefully lifts termites out of their nest with a thin stick. She eats them quickly before they can bite.

Babies

The mother carries her baby until it is nearly four years old. The tuft of white hair on its bottom shows that it is a baby, and reminds the family to treat it gently.

Babies spend many hours playing, just like us. Their pink ears and faces become darker as they grow older.

Growing Up

This six-month-old baby is learning
fast. Perched on her mother's back,
she watches how her uncle eats fruit.

Chimpanzees must also learn how to **communicate** with each other. This young chimp is hooting to let others know where he is.

Getting Angry

Another chimp has bothered this male.
He is making a lot of noise. Look how his
hair is on end!

When chimpanzees show their teeth like this, they are not happy.

Why do you think the mother is angry?

Chimpanzee Facts

- Chimpanzees live for about 40 to 50 years.

- Male chimps can be **aggressive**. They scream, beat the ground with their hands, and throw sticks at each other.

- Chimps eat mainly fruit, leaves and insects. They enjoy meat, and sometimes hunt monkeys and wild pigs.

- Chimps can use tools, like sticks and stones. Very few animals can do this. Chimps can even make a sponge out of leaves and bark. They use it to soak up water for drinking.

- Chimpanzees are in danger. People cut down the forests where they live. Many young chimps are trapped and sold to collectors.

Glossary

aggressive   Someone who fights and shouts is aggressive.

apes   Animals like chimpanzees, with hands and no tails.

communicate   Give others information, and let them know what you think and feel.

grooming   Tidying and cleaning hair and skin.

knuckles   Parts of your fingers that bend.

termite   Insects a bit like ants.

tropical   In the hot and rainy parts of the world.

Index

More Books To Read

Butterworth, Christine and Bailey, Donna. *Chimpanzees*. Austin, Ex: Raintree Steck-Vaughn, 1990.

Gondola, Jane. *The Chimpanzee Family Book*. New York: Simon & Schuster Children's, 1991.

Stone, Lynn. *Chimpanzees*. Vero Beach, Fla.: Rourke, 1990.